DID YOU KNOW?

Contents

About you 2
Around the house 4
Long ago 6
Even longer ago 8
The world and the weather 10
Earth and space 12
Machines, past and present 14
Plant life 16
Animal life .18
Tell the tale 20
Answers 22

Written by Jenny Vaughan
Illustrated by Frank James

Collins Educational
An Imprint of HarperCollinsPublishers

ABOUT YOU

1 A giraffe has more neck bones than a human. True or false?

2 Which has the best sense of smell – a human or a dog?

3 How many tastes can your tongue taste?

4 Which is more sensitive, your nose or your toes?

5 We hear with our ears, but they have another job, too. What is it?

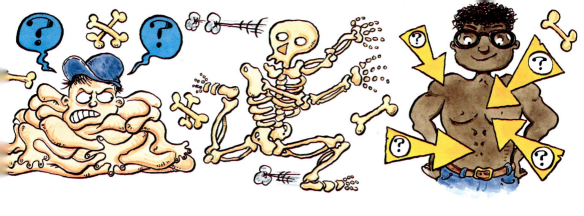

6 Why do some people get hay fever?

7 Where is your funny bone?

8 Why do you shiver when you are cold?

9 Identical twins have the same fingerprints. True or false?

10 Is is healthy to eat chocolate and nothing else?

Answers on page 22

AROUND THE HOUSE

1 Houses are often made from bricks – but what are bricks made from?

2 Poking things into electric sockets is dangerous. Why?

3 When you hang washing out to dry, what happens to the water?

4 If you look at yourself in the bowl of a spoon, you see yourself upside-down. True or false?

5 What is a plumber?

6 Why do we try to keep flies away from our food?
   a) they look horrible
   b) they carry germs
   c) they make a nasty, buzzing noise.

7 What is recycled paper made from?

8 What does it mean when we say food is 'preserved'?

9 Pictures on a television screen are made up of tiny dots in three colours. Some are green. Some are blue. What colour are the others?

10 Why do people put solar panels on the roofs of their houses?

Answers on page 23

LONG AGO

1 In which country in Africa are the pyramids?

2 What is the name of the important river which flows through Egypt?

3 What were the kings of Egypt called?

4 What was the name of the Greek scientist who jumped out of his bath shouting "Eureka!"?

5 In which city can you see a building called the Parthenon?
a) Athens b) London c) Rome.

6 The city of Rome was the capital city of the Roman Empire. It is still a capital, but of which country?

7 Roman roads were long and well-made. Why else were they special?

8 The Romans ruled in parts of Africa. True or false?

9 Where did the Saxons come from?

10 Britain was invaded by people who came across the sea from Norway and Denmark. Who were they?

Answers on page 24

EVEN LONGER AGO

1 Where did the first life begin?
a) on land
b) in the air
c) in the water.

2 If a diplodocus met an elephant, which would be bigger?

3 Pterosaurs could do something that dinosaurs could not. What was it?

4 200 million years ago, would you find an ichthyosaur in the sea or in the air?

5 The dinosaur tyrannosaurus was a vegetarian. True or false?

6 Archaeopteryx is the name for which of the following:
a) a collector of dinosaur fossils
b) the very first kind of bird
c) a swimming dinosaur

7 Why are we certain that no one ever had a pet dinosaur?

8 There were no mammals around in the days of the dinosaurs. True or false?

9 Scientists believe the very first people came from Africa. True or false?

10 What animal alive today is related to the hairy mammoth?

Answers on page 25

THE WORLD AND THE WEATHER

1 Which happens first, thunder or lightning?

2 What name do we give to a river of ice?

3 What are lumps of ice that fall from the sky called?

4 Where is it never dark in the summer?

5 Fog is made up of tiny droplets of water in the air. True or false?

6 What kind of mountain pours out molten rock?

7 It is a huge lump of ice floating in the sea, and can be big enough to sink a ship. What is it called?

8 What is the name for the place where a river begins?

9 Are deserts always sandy?

10 Earthquakes always happen when too many moles and other animals burrow under the ground. True or false?

Answers on page 26

Earth and space

1 What makes the moon shine?

2 What is the nearest star to earth?

3 Would you be north or south of the Equator if water goes down the plughole in a clockwise direction?

4 Why is it impossible for a spaceship to land on Jupiter?

5 What colour is the soil on Mars?

6 What is a meteorite?

7 Why does the moon seem to change shape, night after night?

8 What happens when there is an eclipse of the sun?

9 The earth and the other planets travel around the moon. True or false?

10 Which way does a compass needle always point?

Answers on page 27

MACHINES, PAST AND PRESENT

1 What makes a water wheel turn?

2 The first people to fly went up in a balloon. Which of these kept their balloon inflated?
a) hydrogen gas
b) hot air
c) a team of pigeons.

3 What did the Wright brothers invent?

4 Which sort of fuel do steam engines usually use?
a) petrol b) gas c) coal.

5 What looked odd about the wheels of the penny-farthing bicycle?

6 A tyre usually has ridges on it, called tread. Why?

7 How does a vacuum cleaner lift dirt off the floor?

8 The exhaust from cars can pollute the air. True or false?

9 Some railway lines have electric cables above them. What are they for?

10 Which of these things did Alexander Graham Bell invent?
a) the motor car
b) the telephone
c) the camera.

Answers on page 28

Plant life

1 Why do so many flowers smell sweet?

2 What are the roots of a plant for?

3 Which one of these trees is a conifer?
a) an oak tree
b) an apple tree
c) a fir tree.

4 What is the link between a loaf of bread and grains of wheat?

5 Peas, beans and peanuts are all seeds. True or false?

6 Some kinds of seeds cling to animals' fur. Why do they do this?

7 Which one of these is not a plant?
  a) a wood anemone
  b) a sea anemone
  c) a daffodil.

8 How can you work out how old a tree is after it has been cut down?

9 All plants need soil to grow. True or false?

10 Are tomatoes fruits or vegetables?

Answers on page 29

ANIMAL LIFE

1 Which animal isn't a hunter?
   a) stoat   b) fox
   c) rabbit   d) wild cat.

2 What are male cattle called?

3 How do bees tell each other where to find flowers for food?

4 What kind of animals have six legs and a body in three parts?

5 All snakes have a poisonous bite. True or false?

6 What do hedgehogs do during the winter?

7 How does an earthworm move?

8 Dodos were flightless birds which lived on the island of Mauritius. Why are they now extinct?

9 Lions, tigers, cheetahs, leopards and jaguars are all members of which family of mammals?

10 Which of these animals is an amphibian?
a) frog b) snake c) horse.

Answers on page 30

TELL THE TALE

1 Who left her shoe behind after she had been out dancing?

2 He left Locksley Hall to live in Sherwood Forest with a band of outlaws. Who was he?

3 Who or what was Mowgli?

4 What is the name of the naughty spider who enjoys playing tricks?

5 Who mistook a wolf for her grandmother?

6 What happened when Aladdin rubbed his magic lamp?

7 Who was the owner of the magical chocolate factory that Charlie visited?

8 What happened to the princess who tried to use a spinning wheel, and then pricked her finger?

9 Which bear was named after a railway station?

10 What was the name of Matilda Wormwood's teacher?

Answers on page 31

ANSWERS

About you:

1 False. They are both mammals, and all mammals have seven neck bones, or vertebrae.

2 A dog. The part of its nose which is used for smelling is much bigger than a human's.

3 Four. (Sweet, sour, bitter and salty.)

4 Your toes.

5 To help us keep our balance.

6 They are allergic to pollen or dust.

7 Near your elbow. It is not a bone, but a small bundle of nerves under the surface of the skin.

8 The action of shivering produces heat, which warms you up.

9 False. Everybody's fingerprints are different.

10 No. It would make you ill. You need a variety of foods including fresh fruit and vegetables or meat.

AROUND THE HOUSE:

1 Clay.

2 You might get an electric shock which could burn or kill you.

3 It 'evaporates'. It changes from its liquid form into a gas called 'water vapour'.

4 True. But if you look at the back, you will be the right way up but an odd shape.

5 A person who fits and mend anything to do with water: pipes, taps, etc.

6 b) they carry germs.

7 Waste paper.

8 'Preserving' food stops it from going off. Freezing food is one way of preserving it. Smoking and salting are others.

9 Red.

10 They produce electricity from the sun's rays.

Long ago:

1 Egypt.

2 The Nile.

3 Pharaohs.

4 Archimedes.

5 a) Athens, in Greece. The Parthenon was a temple built in 5BC.

6 Italy.

7 They were straight.

8 True. The Romans ruled for about 700 years.

9 Northern Germany and part of what is now The Netherlands.

10 The Vikings. They invaded Britain between 8AD and 11AD.

EVEN LONGER AGO:

1 c) in the water.

2 a diplodocus. It weighed up to 11 tonnes. African elephants can weigh about 6 tonnes.

3 They could fly.

4 In the sea.

5 False. They were carnivores.

6 b) the very first kind of bird.

7 Dinosaurs died out before humans ever existed.

8 False. Mammals started to exist about 200 million years ago, long before the dinosaurs died out.

9 True. The oldest fossils have been found there.

10 The elephant.

THE WORLD AND THE WEATHER:

1. They happen at the same time. We see the lightning first because the light reaches our eyes faster than the sound of thunder reaches our ears.

2. A glacier.

3. Hailstones.

4. The North Pole; during the winter it is never light.

5. True.

6. A volcano. When it erupts, it pours out lava, which is a molten rock.

7. An iceberg.

8. The source.

9. No. Many deserts are rocky.

10. False. Earthquakes happen when sections of the earth's crust suddenly move.

Earth and Space:

1. The moon reflects light from the sun.

2. The sun. It is 149.6 million kilometres from earth.

3. South. North of the Equator, water goes down the plughole in an anti-clockwise direction.

4. Jupiter is mostly made up of gas and liquid, so it is not solid enough to land on.

5. Red.

6. A lump of rock that falls on earth from space.

7. We can only see the parts of the moon that the sun shines on. The rest is in the earth's shadow. As the moon travels round the earth, the amount of shadow on its surface changes, so the moon appears to change shape.

8. The moon travels in front of the sun, blocking out the sun's light.

9. False. They orbit the sun. The sun and the planets going round it are called the solar system.

10. North.

MACHINES, PAST AND PRESENT:

1 Running water.

2 Hot air.

3 The first aeroplane that actually flew.

4 c) Coal.

5 The front wheel was huge and the back wheel was tiny. The pedals were fixed directly to the front wheel (see page 32).

6 To help the tyre grip the road. Without the tread it might skid.

7 It sucks in air so the dirt comes up with the air.

8 True. Exhaust fumes are one of the main causes of air pollution.

9 They carry electricity, which the trains use to drive their engines.

10 b) The telephone.

PLANT LIFE:

1 To attract insects. They collect nectar and pollen from the flowers. This spreads pollen from flower to flower.

2 They draw up minerals and water for the plant.

3 c) a fir tree. Conifers are trees which have cones.

4 Bread is made from flour, which is made by grinding up grains of wheat.

5 True.

6 Seeds need to disperse or spread. An animal can carry a seed in its coat a long way.

7 b) a sea anemone. This is a kind of animal although it looks like a plant.

8 By counting the number of rings in the trunk. There is one for each year (see page 32).

9 False. Some plants can grow in water, others may grow in sand, in air, on bricks or tissue paper. Plants need water, but they do not need soil.

10 Fruits. Fruits contain seeds, vegetables do not.

Animal life:

1 c) rabbit. Rabbits eat plants.

2 Bulls (see page 32).

3 They move in a certain pattern which shows other bees which way to fly to find the food.

4 Insects.

5 False. Many, such as grass snakes, do not have a poisonous bite.

6 They hibernate because food is scarce.

7 It has tiny bristles on its body which dig into the earth, helping it to burrow.

8 They were all hunted and killed by people. The last one died in 1681.

9 The cat family.

10 a) frog. The snake is a reptile and the horse is a mammal.

Tell the tale:

1. Cinderella left her shoe behind when the clock struck midnight.
2. Robin of Locksley (Robin Hood).
3. A boy who lived in the jungle with the animals in *The Jungle Book* by Rudyard Kipling.
4. Anansi.
5. Red Riding Hood.
6. A magical genie appeared who could grant any wish.
7. Willie Wonka in *Charlie and the Chocolate Factory* by Roald Dahl.
8. She slept for 100 years.
9. Paddington Bear.
10. Miss Jenny Honey in *Matilda* by Roald Dahl.

A tree trunk.

A penny-farthing bicycle.

A bull.